Are you as eager as I am to read this book? Turn the page!

Library of Congress Cataloging-in-Publication Data
Title: Beavers
Description: New York, NY: Children's Press, an imprint of Scholastic Inc., 2020. | Series: Wild Life LOL! | Includes index.
Identifiers: LCCN 2019006052| ISBN 9780531240342 (library binding) | ISBN 9780531234877 (paperback)
Subjects: LCSH: Beavers—Juvenile literature.
Classification: LCC QL737.R632 B435 2020 | DDC 599.37—dc23

Produced by Spooky Cheetah Press

Design by Anna Tunick Tabachnik

Contributing Editor and Jokester: Pamela Chanko

Printed in Heshan, China 62

1 2 3 4 5 6 7 8 9 10 R 29 28 27 26 25 24 23 22 21 20

Scholastic Inc., 557 Broadway, New York, NY 10012.

Photographs ©: cover, spine, and throughout: George Lepp/Getty Images; cover speech bubbles and throughout: Astarina/Shutterstock; cover speech bubbles and throughout: pijama61/iStockphoto; back cover and throughout: Jody Ann/Shutterstock; 2: Robert McGouey/Getty Images; 4: Robert McGouey/Getty Images; 5 left: All-Silhouettes.com; 5 right: Irina Iarovaia/Dreamstime; 6-7: Chase Dekker/Shutterstock; 8-9: Konrad Wothe/Minden Pictures; 10: Thomas & Pat Leeson/Science Source; 11 left: Outdoorsman/Dreamstime; 11 center: yarb1959/iStockphoto; 11 right: Daniel J. Cox/Getty Images; 12: stanley45/iStockphoto; 13 left: Donald M. Jones/Minden Pictures; 13 right: John Webster/Getty Images; 14-15: Robert B McGouey/age fotostock; 16: Francis Photo/age fotostock; 17: De Agostini Picture Library/Getty Images; 18: Jillian Cooper/iStockphoto; 19 top left: Christy Davies/EyeEm/Getty Images; 19 top right: Bernard Jaubert/Getty Images; 19 bottom left: Julia Podus/Shutterstock; 19 bottom right: Chris002/Shutterstock; 20-21: Rosanne Tackaberry/Alamy Images; 22: Robert McGouey/Wildlife/Alamy Images; 23 left: Ingo Arndt/Minden Pictures; 23 right: Thomas & Pat Leeson/Science Source; 24-25: Mark Mauno/Flickr; 25 bottom right: Robert McGouey/Getty Images; 26 left: Peter Newark American Pictures/Bridgeman Images; 26 right: Chris Howes/Wild Places Photography/Alamy Images; 27 left: Gregory K Scott/Getty Images; 28 left: legna69/iStockphoto; 28 top: Joel Sartore/National Geographic/Getty Images; 29 left: Tap10/Shutterstock; 29 center: Joel Sartore/Getty Images; 29 right: Volga2012/iStockphoto; 30 map: Jim McMahon/Mapman®; 30 bottom: Robert McGouey/Getty Images; 31 top: Chase Dekker/Shutterstock; 32: Danita Delimont/Getty Images.

TABLE OF CONTENTS

Meet the Busy Beaver 4
Life in the Pond 6
A Beaver's Body 8
Predator Slapdown 10
Building a Dam 12
A Beaver's Family 14
Welcome Home! 16
Let's Eat! 18
Time to Take Off 20
Beaver Babies 22
Giants from the Past 24
Beavers and People 26

This is all about me, FUR real?

Beaver Cousins 28
The Wild Life 30
Index 32
About This Book 32

MEET THE BUSY BEAVER

Are you ready to be amazed and amused? Keep reading. This book will give you plenty of facts to chew on!

I WOOD like to have whiter teeth. May I borrow your toothbrush?

At a Glance

Where do they live? Beavers live in lakes, ponds, and streams. They live across the United States.

What do they do? Beavers are builders. They cut down trees to make dams and homes.

What do they eat? Beavers are plant-eaters.

What do they look like? Beavers are furry. They have long front teeth and flat, wide tails.

How big are they?

HINT: You're bigger. Check this out:

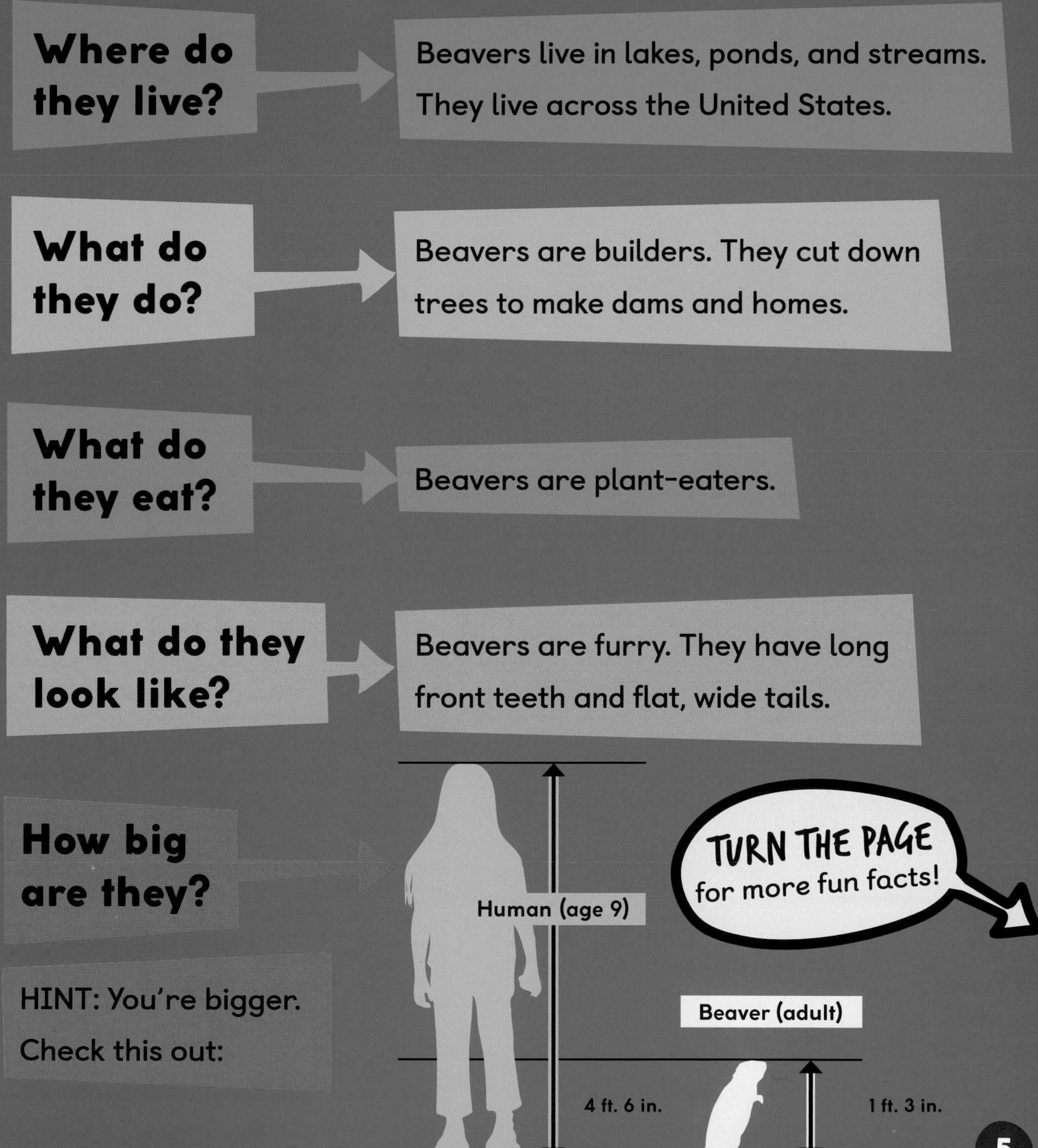

LIFE IN THE POND

Beavers are semi-aquatic. They spend some time on land and some in water. Their teeth are key to their **survival**.

That's *So* Bunny!
Both beavers and bunnies have long front teeth that never stop growing! Both animals have to chew on things to trim them down!

Do Beavers Need a Dentist?
Nah. Beavers' teeth might look really dirty, but they're not. A coating that contains iron makes a beaver's teeth strong—and orange!

WACKY FACT: Beavers work mostly at night.

Here, Kitty Kitty Kitty!
An adult beaver weighs from 30 to 60 pounds. The smallest is about three times the size of a house cat.

LOL!
How does a beaver get onto the internet?
It LOGS on!

survival: the act of continuing to live or exist

A BEAVER'S BODY

Beavers' bodies are built for swimming. Check it out!

THAT'S EXTREME! A beaver can hold its breath for up to 15 minutes.

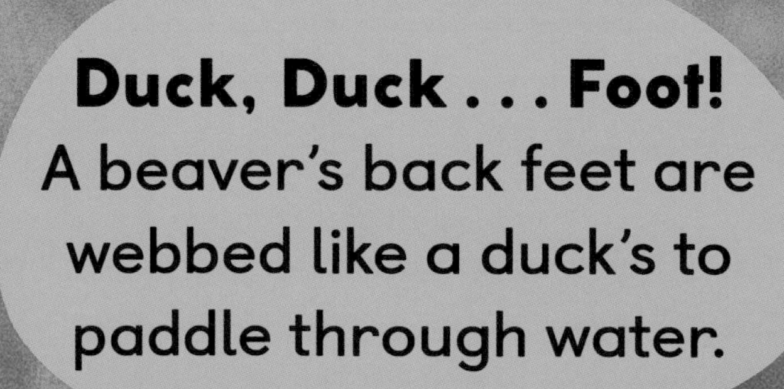

Duck, Duck . . . Foot!
A beaver's back feet are webbed like a duck's to paddle through water.

So Cozy . . .
The beaver's furry coat keeps it warm in the chilly water.

Built-In Swim Goggles
Beavers have an extra pair of see-through eyelids so they can see underwater.

You'll never catch me doing the dog paddle. I do the beaver paddle!

LOL!
Knock, knock!
Who's there?
Beaver E.
Beaver E. who?
Beaver E. Quiet. I'm playing hide-and-seek!

PREDATOR SLAPDOWN

SPLAT!

That's what it sounds like when a beaver slaps its broad, flat tail on the water. The loud splash scares away **predators**, such as coyotes, bears, and wolves.

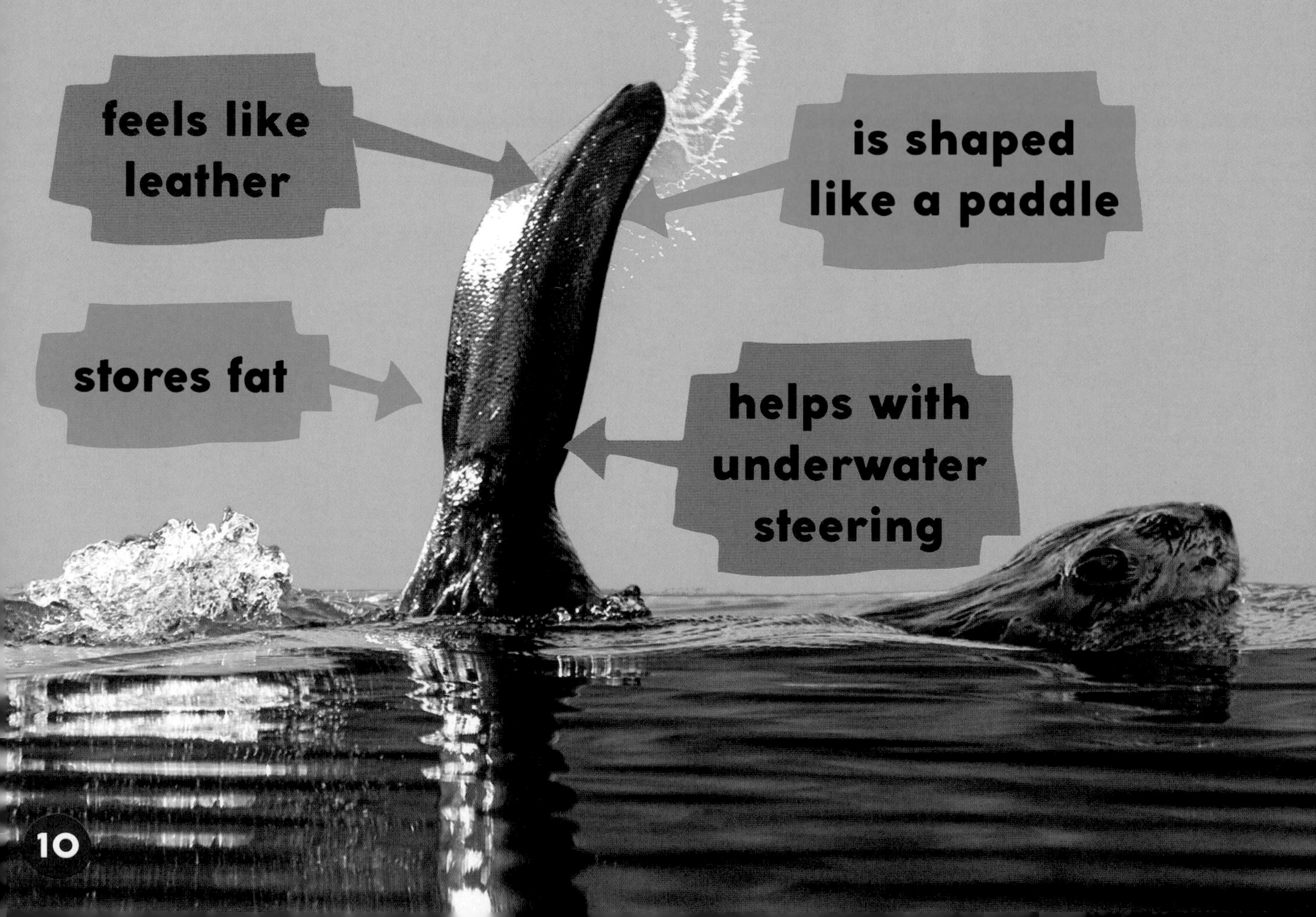

predators: animals that hunt other animals for food

BUILDING A DAM

Beavers look for a pond or lake to live in. If they cannot find one, they may create their own in a slow-moving river! Here's how.

Well, tree, it's been nice GNAW-ing you!

1

A beaver uses its strong teeth to chew through the base of a tree. *Chomp . . . chomp . . . craaaack!* The beaver bites through the log to make smaller pieces.

WACKY FACT: The world's largest dam is over half a mile long! Scientists think beavers have been adding to it since the 1970s.

2

The beaver grabs one of the pieces with its teeth and drags the wood into the river. It swims with the small log in its mouth to the dam it is building.

3

The busy beaver builds the dam using this log and others, as well as mud, leaves, and stones. The dam will hold back the river to form a new pond.

A BEAVER'S FAMILY

Beavers live in a big family group called a **colony**. Each colony can have as many as 12 members!

Kits
Beaver babies are called kits. All the youngsters in a colony are under three years old.

Are we done with our swim lesson yet?!

Dad
This is the father of all the baby beavers in the colony.

LOL!
Where do beavers keep their money?
In the riverbank!

Mom
The mother beaver is the head of the family. She is in charge!

colony: a large group of animals that live together

WELCOME HOME!

The beaver family shares a big house called a lodge.

outside view

Anybody Home?

This is a lodge. From outside, it looks like a pile of sticks.

LOL!
What did the beaver say to the twig?
I'm STICK-ing with you!

WACKY FACT:
A beaver's lips close behind its front teeth so it can carry things underwater without drowning!

Keeping It Fresh

A hole in the top of the lodge lets stale air escape.

THAT'S EXTREME!

In winter, when a pond freezes, beavers travel in and out beneath the ice.

Hold Your Breath

The only way to get inside the lodge is through underwater tunnels.

Wipe Your Feet

The floor is built higher than the water, so it stays dry. When the kits are old enough, they help keep the floor clean.

LET'S EAT!

Beavers eat different parts of plants and trees. They mostly nibble on **bark**, leaves, twigs, and roots. Sometimes beavers store food in their lodges.

THAT'S EXTREME!
Beavers eat their own poop! That's how they get the most from their food—by eating it twice!

WACKY FACT:
April 7 is International Beaver Day.

LEAF-ing so soon? But it's suppertime!

bark: the tough outer covering on the stems of plants

maple trees
linden trees
These are some of a beaver's favorite meals.
water lilies
poplar trees

TIME TO TAKE OFF

When a beaver is about two years old, it is ready to leave home. It's time for the beaver to start a family of its own!

THAT'S EXTREME!
Beavers squirt a smelly oil from under their tails. They do that to leave their scent on mud piles near their ponds.

1

The Search

The beaver wanders around looking for a pond where it can build a lodge—or build a dam to form a pond.

WACKY FACT:
People used to use the oil beavers squirt on the mud to make perfume!

2

This Stinks!

The beaver finds smelly piles of mud. They've been left behind by other beavers. The message: This pond is taken.

3

Home, Sweet Home

The beaver doesn't stop until it finds its own place. Then it creates its own mud pile and squirts oil on the mound!

BEAVER BABIES

In late spring it is time for the busy beaver to start its own family.

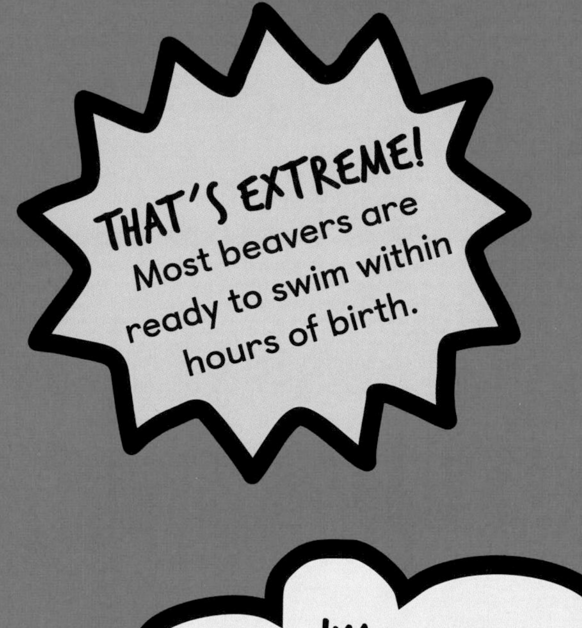

1

Meet Your Match

When a male beaver finds a female, they may wrestle for fun in the water. If they decide to become a pair, they rub noses. That's how beavers kiss.

WACKY FACT:
Beavers grow super fast! They reach 25 pounds in a year's time. That's as much as a two-year-old child weighs.

Look, kits! It's not that hard if you just STICK to it!

2

Here Come the Kits

In April, May, or June of the next year, the kits arrive. A beaver can have two to five kits. Newborns have fluffy hair and can fit in a grown-up's hand. Their front teeth are already long!

3

Beaver School

One of the first things beavers learn is to leave the house to poop! When the kit is one year old, its mom starts giving it chores. At about $1\frac{1}{2}$ years old, the kit learns how to build.

GIANTS FROM THE PAST

Many thousands of years ago, giant beavers roamed Earth. They looked like today's beavers, but they were huge! Scientists know what they looked like because they have found **fossils** like this one.

WACKY FACT: This fossil was found in Indiana in the 1800s.

Long Tail
The giant beaver had a long tailbone like a modern beaver's.

fossils: plants or animals from millions of years ago preserved as rock

Bear or Beaver?
The giant beaver was almost as big as a black bear.

Huge Teeth
The giant beaver's front teeth were almost as long as your hand.

BEAVERS AND PEOPLE

We have a long history together!

About 12,000 years ago

There were millions of beavers in North America. Some Native American tribes, or nations, hunted beavers. They took only what they could use.

Mid-1800s

Settlers in North America hunted many beavers to make hats and other items to sell around the world. The number of beavers dropped to only thousands.

Mid-1900s

Humans began to understand how important beavers are. For example, when they create a new pond, other animals, like ducks, go to live there, too.

Today

Millions of beavers once again live in the wild in the United States. Conservation laws help to protect beavers and the places where they live.

Beaver Cousins

Beavers belong to a family of animals called rodents. All rodents have two large front teeth, which they use to gnaw, or chew. Check out the beaver's closest cousins. All of them are rodents.

We have long front teeth, too. We dig tunnels underground, not underwater.

gophers

Like beavers, we have long front teeth, but we don't build dams. We build nests.

These guys look really familiar!

squirrels

Please note: Animals are not shown to scale.

We are tiny rats that live in the desert.

kangaroo rats

We are the largest rodents in the world. Like beavers, we have webbed feet so we can paddle in water.

We are wild animals, but we are also kept as pets.

guinea pigs

capybaras

The Wild Life

Look at this map of the world. The areas in red show where beavers live today: most of North America and parts of South America, Europe, and Asia. We want beavers to continue having **habitats** to live in. Otherwise, one day there might not be any red left on this map.

habitats: the places where a plant or an animal makes its home

What Can You Do?

1

Beavers need a peaceful habitat to live in.

If you see a beaver dam or lodge . . . leave it alone!

2

Trees provide homes for beavers and other animals, and clean air for us to breathe. By protecting trees, you are protecting beavers, too!

Write on both sides of your paper, and ask the adults around you to use reusable lunch bags instead of paper ones. Fewer trees will need to be cut down!

3

Litter and pollution are harmful to all living things, including beavers. By creating less **waste**, you are helping beavers and our planet.

Learn about and always practice the three Rs: reduce, reuse, and recycle.

waste: anything we throw away or don't use

INDEX

colony 14–15
dam 12–13
eyes 9
feet 8
food 18–19
fossils 24–25
fur 9, 26
International Beaver Day 18
kits 14–15, 17, 22–23
lodge 16–17, 18, 20
oil 20, 21
semi-aquatic 6
starting a family 22–23
swimming 8-9, 13, 22
tail 10, 20, 24
teeth 6, 12, 13, 16, 23, 25
threats 10, 11, 26
weight 7, 22

ABOUT THIS BOOK

This book is a laugh-out-loud early-grade adaptation of *Beavers* by Moira Rose Donohue. *Beavers* was originally published by Scholastic as part of its Nature's Children series in 2019.